Gustav HOLST
A FUGAL CONCERTO
H. 152
Edited by
Richard W. Sargeant, Jr.

Study Score
Partitur

SERENISSIMA MUSIC, INC.

CONTENTS

1. Moderato 3

2. Adagio 10

3. Allegro 14

ORCHESTRA

Flute

Oboe

Violins I

Violins II

Violas

Violoncellos

Double Basses

Duration: ca. 8 minutes

Premiere: May 17, 1923
Ann Arbor, Michigan
University of Michigan President's House
Chicago Symphony Orchestra members / Frederick Stock

This score is an entirely new edition based on the
composer's holograph and the first edition score and parts
which was engraved by the editor.

Printed in the USA

A FUGAL CONCERTO
H.152
1.

Gustav Holst
Edited by Richard W. Sargeant, Jr.

* can be substituted with solo violins

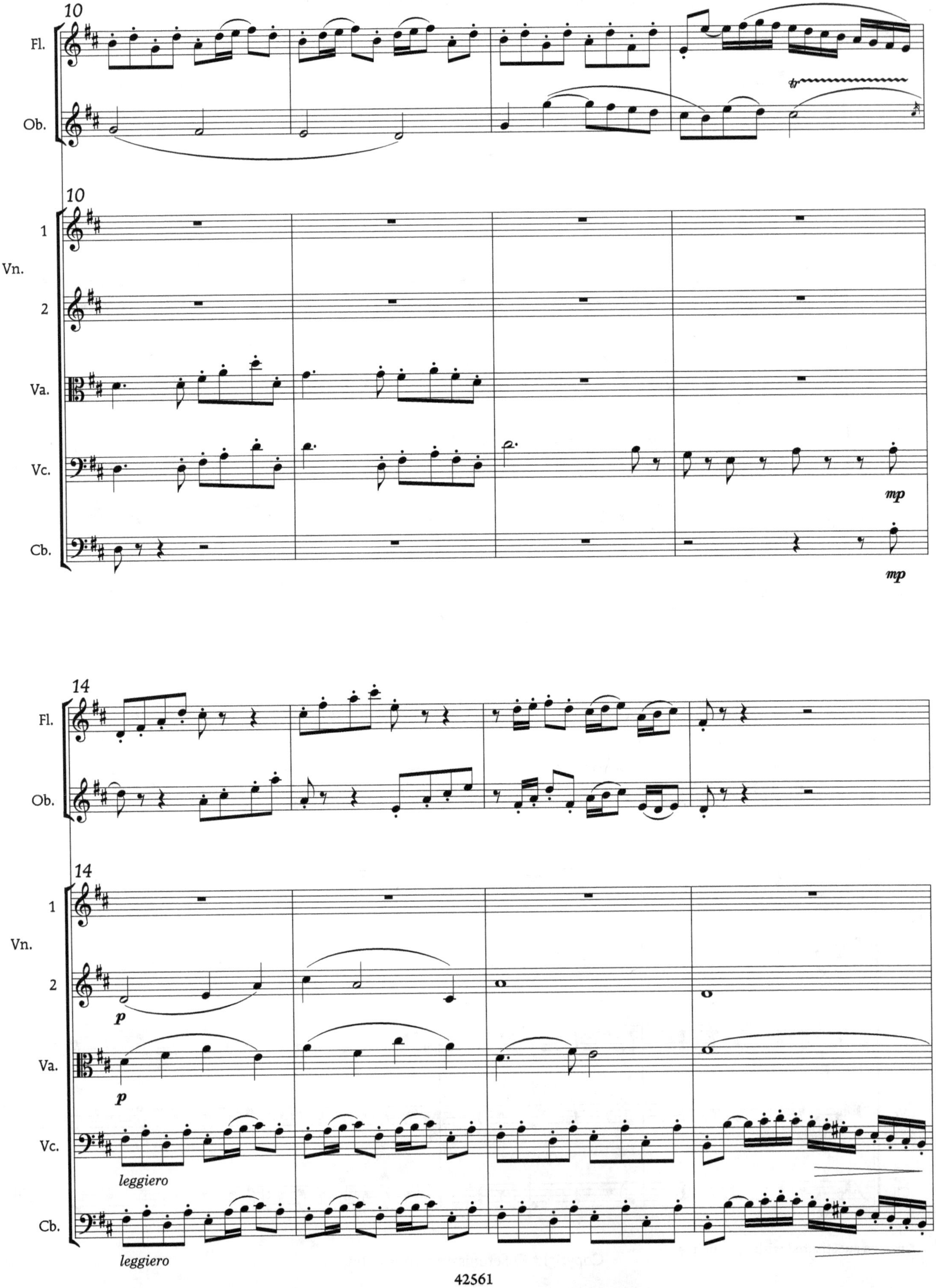
10
Fl.
tr
Ob.
10
1
Vn.
2
Va.
Vc.
mp
Cb.
mp
14
Fl.
Ob.
14
1
Vn.
2
p
Va.
p
Vc.
leggiero
Cb.
leggiero

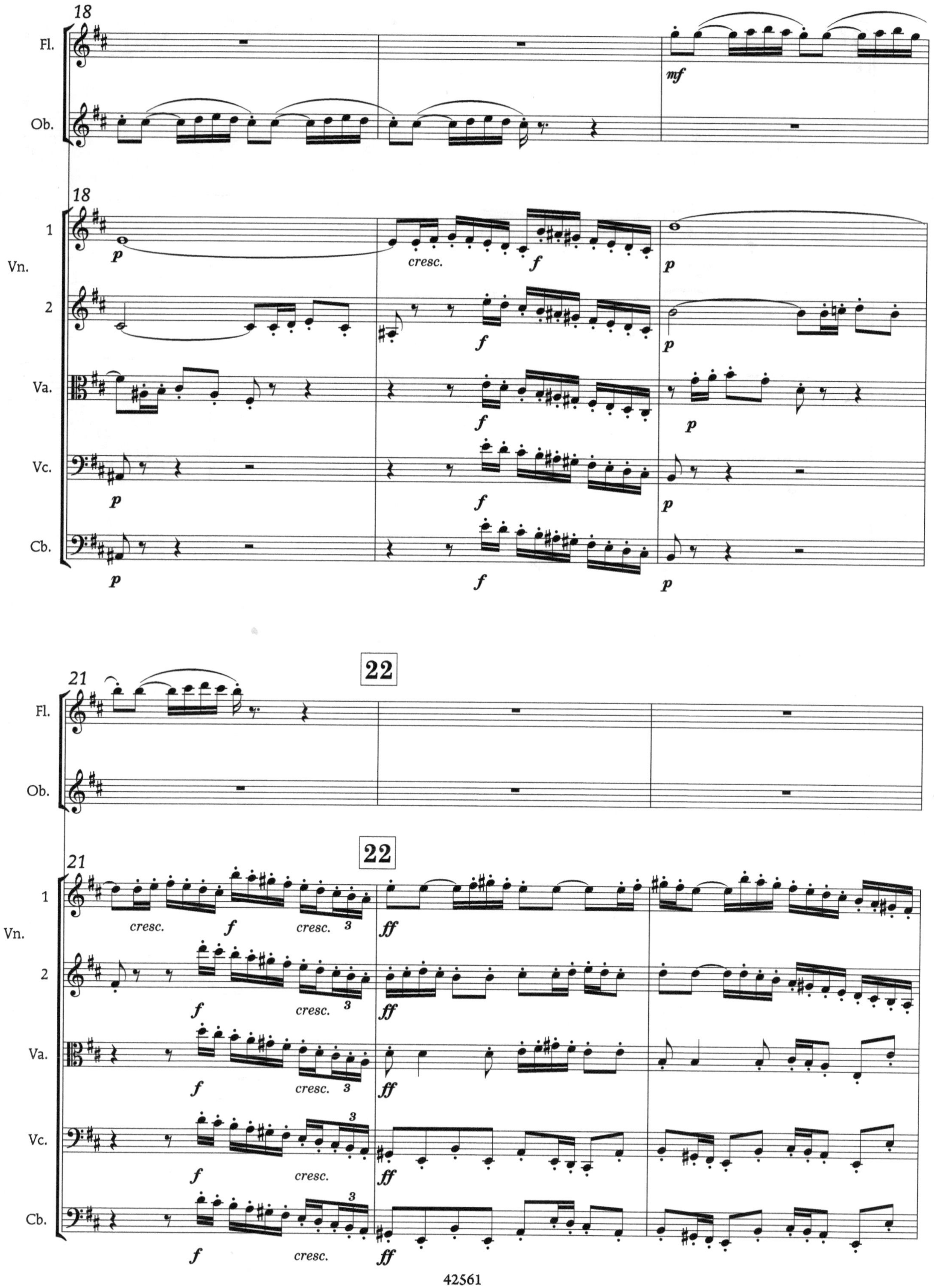
18
Fl.
Ob.
mf
18
Vn.
1
2
Va.
Vc.
Cb.
p
cresc.
f
p
21
22
cresc.
f
cresc.
ff

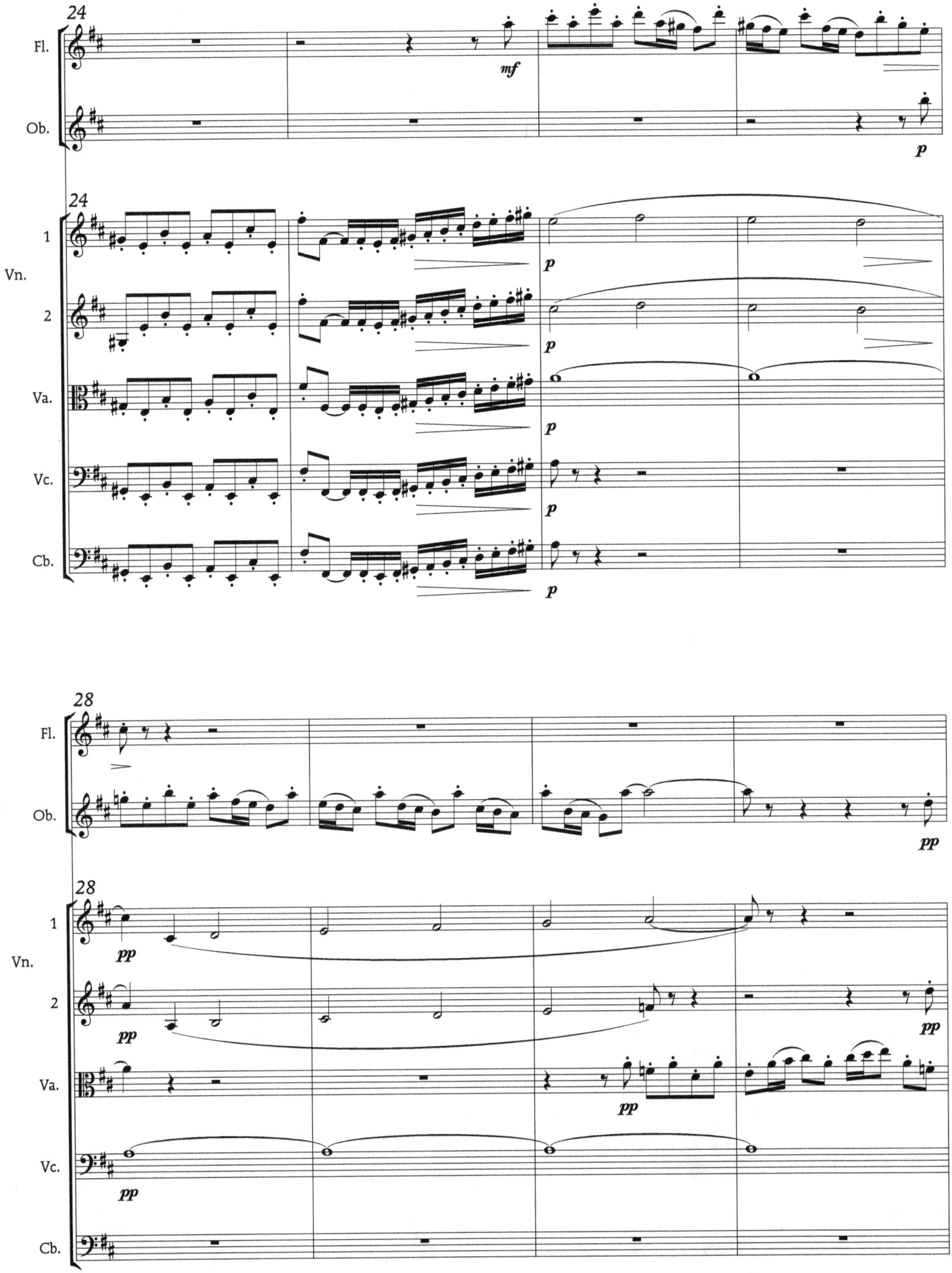
24
Fl.
Ob.
mf
p
24
1
Vn.
2
Va.
Vc.
Cb.
p
28
Fl.
Ob.
pp
28
1
Vn.
2
Va.
Vc.
Cb.
pp

2.

3.

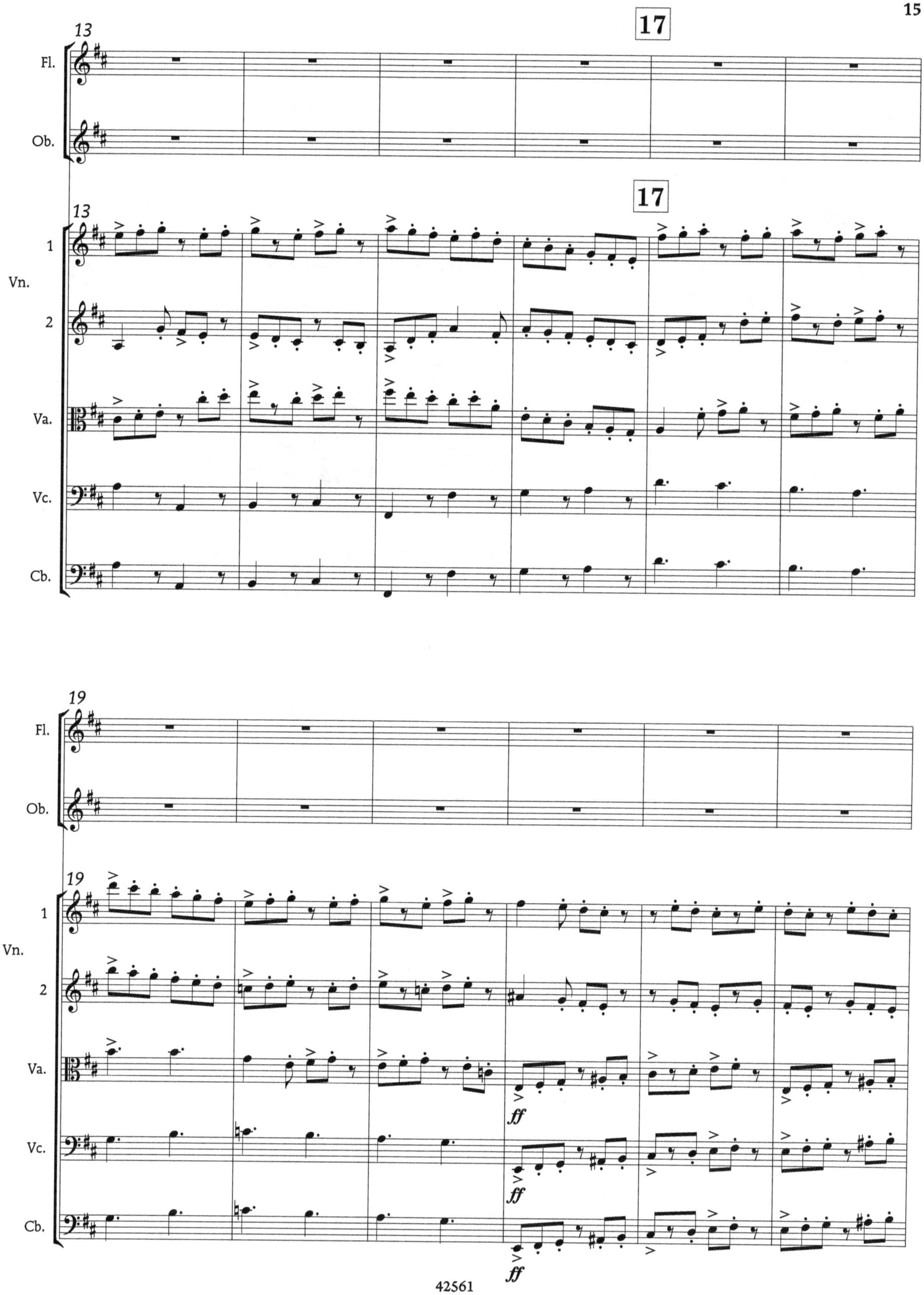
17
13
Fl.
Ob.
17
13
Vn.
1
2
Va.
Vc.
Cb.
19
Fl.
Ob.
19
Vn.
1
2
Va.
Vc.
Cb.
ff
ff
ff

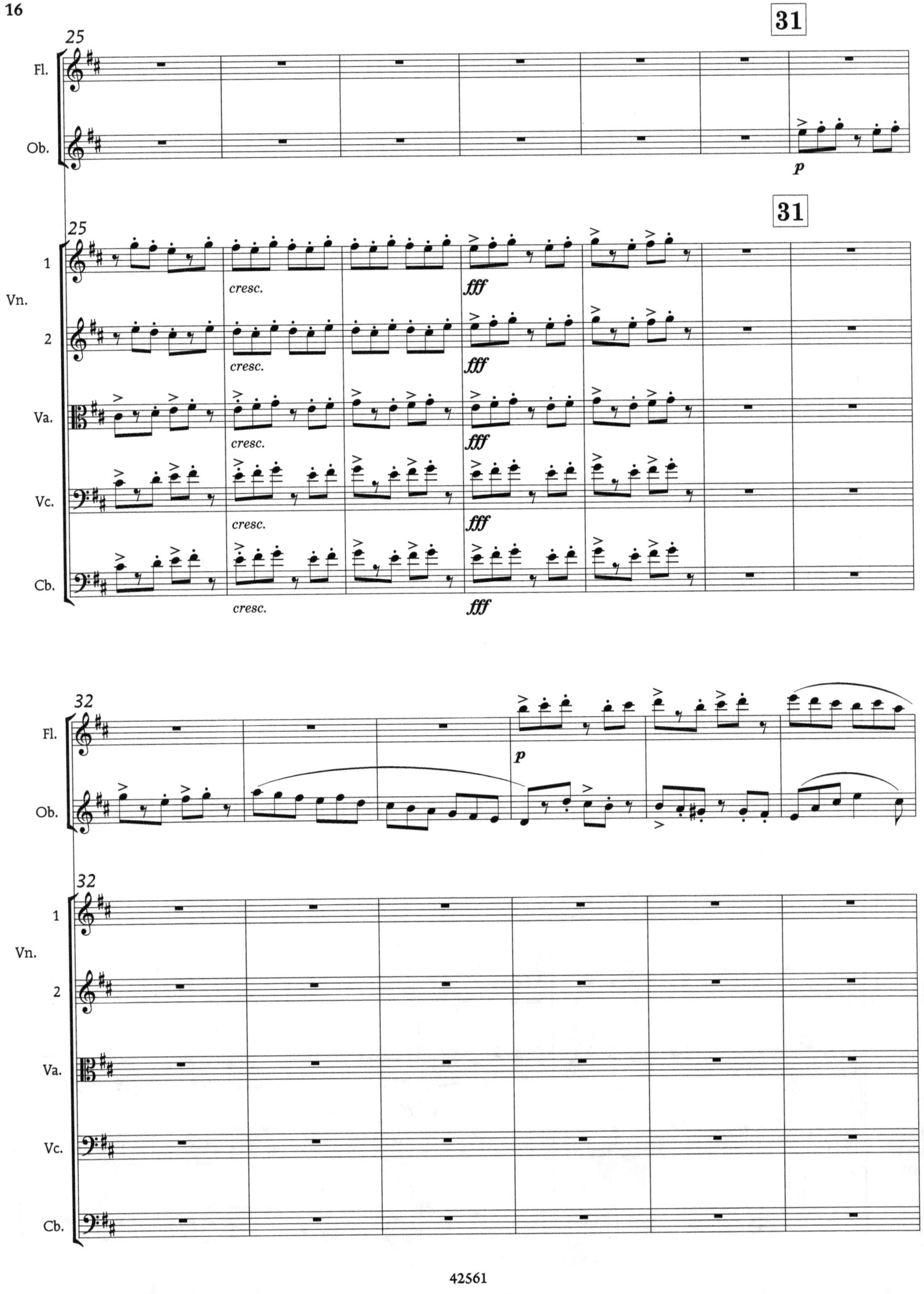
25
31
Fl.
Ob.
p
Vn.
1
2
Va.
Vc.
Cb.
cresc.
fff
32

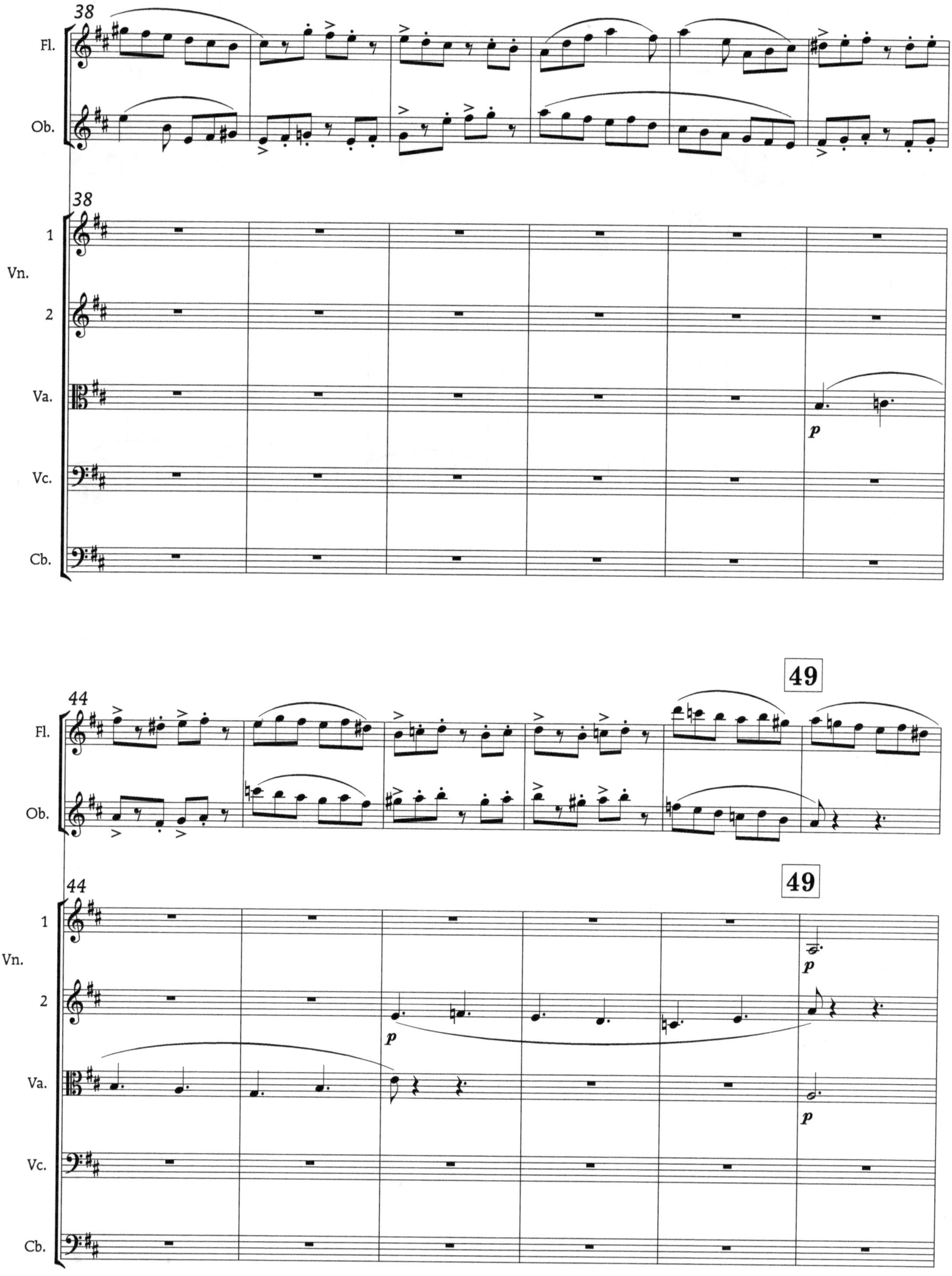
38
Fl.
Ob.
38
1
Vn.
2
Va.
p
Vc.
Cb.
44
49
Fl.
Ob.
44
49
1
Vn.
p
2
p
Va.
p
Vc.
Cb.

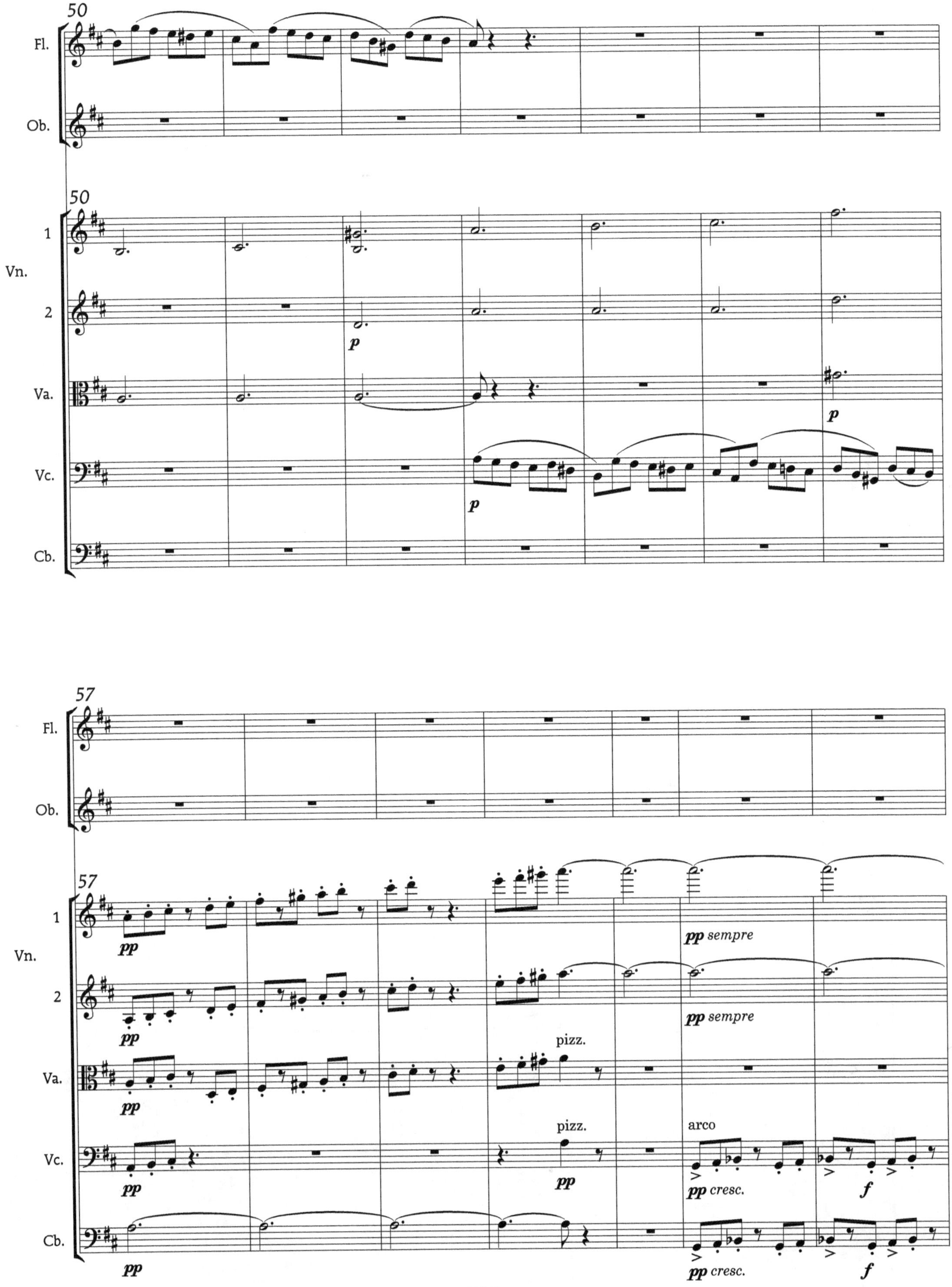
50
Fl.
Ob.
50
Vn.
1
2
p
Va.
p
Vc.
p
Cb.
57
Fl.
Ob.
57
Vn.
1
pp
pp sempre
2
pp
pp sempre
Va.
pp
pizz.
Vc.
pp
pizz.
pp
arco
pp cresc.
f
Cb.
pp
pp cresc.
f

22

42561

* If preferred, this passage may be played by one or more cellos, the basses entering at 119 on the sustained note.

www.ingramcontent.com/pod-product-compliance
Lightning Source LLC
Chambersburg PA
CBHW081026040426
42444CB00014B/3368